Look out for Bingo

Story by Jenny Giles

Illustrations by Pat Reynolds

Sam said,

"I'm hot, Mom.

Can I play in the water?"

"Yes, Sam," said Mom.

"Away you go."

"I like playing
in the water, Mom,"
said Sam.
"Look at me!
I can run in and out
of the water."

"Look at Bingo, Mom,"
said Sam.
"He likes playing
in the water, too.
He likes running after me."

Sam said,

"I'm going to get dry.

Where is my towel?"

"Here you are," said Mom.

"I will help you get dry."

"I'm all dry," said Sam.
"I'm going inside
to get dressed."

"Sam! Look out for Bingo,"
said Mom.
"He is running after you!
Bingo can not go inside.
He is all wet!"

"Go away, Bingo!" said Sam.
"Go away!
You can not come inside
with me.
Oh, Mom! Look at Bingo!"

"And look at me!

I'm all wet again."